PROVINCES

Works in English by Czeslaw Milosz

The Captive Mind
Seizure of Power
Postwar Polish Poetry: An Anthology
Native Realm: A Search for Self-Definition
Selected Poems by Zbigniew Herbert
(translated by Czeslaw Milosz and Peter Dale Scott)
The History of Polish Literature
Selected Poems
Mediterranean Poems by Aleksander Wat
(translated by Czeslaw Milosz)
Emperor of the Earth: Modes of Eccentric Vision
Bells in Winter
The Witness of Poetry
The Issa Valley
Visions from San Francisco Bay
The Separate Notebooks
The Land of Ulro
Unattainable Earth
The Collected Poems 1931–1987
With the Skin: Poems of Aleksander Wat
(translated and edited by Czeslaw Milosz and Leonard Nathan)
Provinces

CZESLAW MILOSZ

PROVINCES

TRANSLATED BY

THE AUTHOR

AND ROBERT HASS

THE ECCO PRESS

NEW YORK

The Ecco Press
26 West 17th Street
New York, NY 10011
Published simultaneously in Canada by
Penguin Books Canada Ltd., Ontario
Printed in the United States of America
First Edition

Grateful acknowledgment is made to the editors of the following publications in which
some of these poems first appeared: Antæus; Humanities; The New Yorker, in which
"Creating the World," "Gathering Apricots," "Incarnated," "In Music," "Mr.
Hanusevich," "On A Beach," "Reconciliation," "The Thistle, The Nettle," and "Youth"
appeared; The New York Times Magazine, in which "Blacksmith Shop" appeared, in a
slightly altered version and under the title "My Lithuanian Childhood: A Smithy"; The
Partisan Review; The Threepenny Review; and ZYZZYVA.

Library of Congress Cataloging-in-Publication Data
Miłosz, Czesław.
Provinces / by Czesław Miłosz. — 1st ed.
p.   cm.
Translated from the Polish: $19.95
1. Miłosz, Czesław—Translations into English.
I. Title.
PG7158.M553A2 1991   891.8'517—dc20   91-3685   CIP
ISBN 0-88001-317-6

The text of this book is set in Janson

CONTENTS

PROVINCES

BLACKSMITH SHOP

I liked the bellows operated by rope.
A hand or foot pedal—I don't remember which.
But that blowing, and the blazing of the fire!
And a piece of iron in the fire, held there by tongs,
Red, softened for the anvil,
Beaten with a hammer, bent into a horseshoe,
Thrown in a bucket of water, sizzle, steam.

And horses hitched to be shod,
Tossing their manes; and in the grass by the river
Plowshares, sledge runners, harrows waiting for repair

At the entrance, my bare feet on the dirt floor,
Here, gusts of heat; at my back, white clouds.
I stare and stare. It seems I was called for this:
To glorify things just because they are.

ADAM AND EVE

Adam and Eve were reading about a monkey in a bath,
Who jumped into the tub, imitating her mistress
And started to turn faucets: Aï, boiling hot!
The lady arrives running, in a robe, her white breasts
Huge, with a blue vein, dangle.
She rescues the monkey, sits at her dressing table,
Calls for her maid, it's time to go to church.

And not only about that were Adam and Eve reading,
Resting a book on their naked knees.
Those castles! Those palaces! Those towering cities!
Planetary airfields between pagodas!
They looked at each other, smiled,
Though uncertainly (you will be, you will know)
And the hand of Eve reached for the apple.

EVENING

An instant of low white clouds before the rising of the moon,
Perfectly immobile on the line of the sea.
The apricot translucence with edges of ash
Darkens, wanes, sets into gray vermillion.

Who is seeing this? The one who doubts his existence.
He strides along the beach, wants to dwell in memory
And to no avail. He is irretrievable, like clouds.
Lungs, liver, sex, not me, not mine.

Masks, wigs, buskins, be with me!
Transform me, take me to a gaudy stage
So that for a moment I can believe I am!

O hymn, O palinode, melopoea,
Sing with my lips, you stop and I perish!

And thus he slowly sinks into the night
Okeanic. No longer held here
By sunrises or the rising of the moon.

CREATING THE WORLD

Celestials at the Board of Projects burst into laughter
For one of them has designed a hedgehog,
Another, not to be left behind, a soprano:
Eyelashes, a bust, and ringlets, plenty of ringlets.

It is superb fun in the ocean of seething energy,
Among bursts and clacks announcing electric currents.
Buckets of proto-colors gurgle, proto-brushes labor,
A mighty whirl of almost galaxies beyond nearly windows
And pure radiance that has never experienced clouds.

They blow conches, somersault in proto-space,
In their realm of archetypes, the seventh heaven.
The earth is practically ready, its rivers sparkle,
Forests cover it, and every single creature
Waits for its name. Thunder strolls the horizon
But the herds in the grass do not lift their heads.

Towns come to be, narrow streets,
A chamberpot poured out a window, laundry.
And immediately freeways to the airport,
A monument at crossroads, a park, a stadium
For thousands when they get up and roar: Goal!

To invent length, width, height,
Two times two and the force of gravity
Would be quite enough, but on top of it, panties
With lace, a hippopotamus, the beak of a toucan,
A chastity belt with its terrible teeth,

A hammerhead shark, a visored helmet,
Plus time, that is, a division into was and will be.

Gloria, gloria, sing objects called to being.
Hearing them, Mozart sits down at the pianoforte
And composes music which had been ready
Before he himself was born in Salzburg.

If only it all could last, but no way.
It iridesces, passes, turns inside a soap-bubble
Together with an invocation Celestials address to the mortals:

"Oh, dizzy tribe, how not to look at you with pity!
Your bright rags, your dances
Seemingly profligate but in truth pathetic,
Mirrors in which you leave a face with earrings,
Painted eyelids, eyelashes with mascara.
Oh, to have so little, nothing except feasts of love!
How feeble your defense against the abyss!"

And the sun rises and the sun sets,
And the sun rises and the sun sets
While they go on running, running.

LINNAEUS

He was born in 1707 at 1:00 a.m. on May 23rd,
when spring was in beautiful bloom, and cuckoo
had just announced the coming of summer.
From Linnaeus's biography

Green young leaves. A cuckoo. Echo.
To get up at four in the morning, to run to the river
Which steams, smooth under the rising sun.
A gate is open, horses are running,
Swallows dart, fish splash. And did we not begin with an
    overabundance
Of glitterings and calls, pursuits and trills?
We lived every day in hymn, in rapture,
Not finding words, just feeling it is too much.

He was one of us, happy in our childhood.
He would set out with his botanic box
To gather and to name, like Adam in the garden
Who did not finish his task, expelled too early.
Nature has been waiting for names ever since:
On the meadows near Uppsala, white, at dusk
Platanthera is fragrant, he called it *bifolia*.
Turdus sings in a spruce thicket, but is it *musicus*?
That must remain the subject of dispute.
And the botanist laughed at a little perky bird
For ever *Troglodytes troglodytes L.*

He arranged three kingdoms into a system.
Animale. Vegetale. Minerale.
He divided: classes, orders, genuses, species.
"How manifold are Thy works, O Jehovah!"
He would sing with the psalmist. Rank, number, symmetry
Are everywhere, praised with a clavecin
And violin, scanned in Latin hexameter.

We have since had the language of marvel: atlases.
A tulip with its dark, mysterious inside,
Anemones of Lapland, a water lily, an iris
Faithfully portrayed by a scrupulous brush.
And a bird in foliage, russet and dark blue,
Never flies off, retained
On the page with an ornate double inscription.

We were grateful to him. In the evenings at home
We contemplated colors under a kerosene lamp
With a green shade. And what there, on earth,
Was unattainable, over much, passing away, perishing,
Here we could love, safe from loss.

May his household, orangery, the garden
In which he grew plants from overseas
Be blessed with peace and well-being.
To China and Japan, America, Australia,
Sailing-ships carried his disciples;
They would bring back gifts: seeds and drawings.
And I, who in this bitter age deprived of harmony
Am a wanderer and a gatherer of visible forms,
Envying them, bring to him my tribute—
A verse imitating the classical ode.

IN MUSIC

Wailing of a flute, a little drum.
A small wedding cortege accompanies a couple
Going past clay houses on the street of a village.
In the dress of the bride much white satin.
How many pennies put away to sew it, once in a lifetime.
The dress of the groom black, festively stiff.
The flute tells something to the hills, parched, the color of deer.
Hens scratch in dry mounds of manure.

I have not seen it, I summoned it listening to music.
The instruments play for themselves, in their own eternity.
Lips glow, agile fingers work, so short a time.
Soon afterwards the pageant sinks into the earth.
But the sound endures, autonomous, triumphant,
For ever visited by, each time returning,
The warm touch of cheeks, interiors of houses,
And particular human lives
Of which the chronicles make no mention.

INCARNATED

In that country he was an officer of cavalry.
He used to frequent good families, even the countess P.
He had boots well polished, a breakfast served
By his orderly, a smart boy from a village.
Girls. More of them than anywhere, the garrison was huge.
Some of them on their own, in rented rooms,
Others in the care of a polite madame
Who greets you under a pink lamp shade
And recommends the hot Irma, the milkwhite Katherine.
A horse dances under him at a review, bells ring,
The clergy strolls in a procession, children pour a powder of
    flowers.
Life there was as it should be. The seasons
Decked the streets with brightness, with the copper of leaves,
    with white.
Peasants from the neighborhood, in sheepskin overcoats
Belted with colorful wool, in bast shoes,
Thongs on the leggings, displayed their products.
Nothing beyond that can be said. He lived, once,
On the pages of chronicles, under a different wind,
Under a different conjunction of stars, though on the same
Earth which, as they say, is a goddess.

MISTER HANUSEVICH

Hanusevich wants Nina. But why? Why?
He has tantrums, blubbers when drunk.
Nina laughs. Is he not funny?
Fat and all nerves, he has big ears
And flaps them, a real elephant.

A dark-blue cloud stands over San Francisco
When I drive along Grizzly Peak,
And far out, beyond the Golden Gate, the ocean gleamed.

Aï, my dead of long ago! Aï, Hanusevich, aï, Nina!
Nobody remembers you, nobody knows about you.

Hanusevich had his estate somewhere near Minsk.
The region was taken by the Bolsheviks, so he lives in Wilno.
When he was young, his mommy let him have flings.
He caroused with chanteuses, pretended to be a big shot,
Would send telegrams in Russian: *"Arriving with ladies*
Meet with music troikas champagne"
And a signature: *Count Bobrinskii.*

Chanteuses. I see now their satin underskirts
And black panties with lace. Breasts, too big, too small,
Worries, touching themselves in mirrors, tardy menses.
Later on they changed into *sestritsas*[1] in the windows of
    hospital trains
(On their brows, bound with a veil, the sign of the red cross).

[1]*Russian military nurse in World War I.*

Nina is not for Hanusevich. Look how she walks.
She rolls from side to side, like a sailor.
A whole year in the saddle, in a cavalry regiment.[2]
What sort of marriageable young lady is she?

What did you find in her, Mister Hanusevich
That you got so romantic? Always pretending,
Perhaps you adorned her with your fantasies.
And, it is true, your funny ears
Nearly transparent, with red veins,
Move, and in your eyes, nearly always, fright.

Once upon a time there was Hanusevich. And there was Nina.
Once only, from the beginning till the end of the world.
It is I who perform, late, this ceremonial wedding.
And around me striped, emerald-eyed beasts,
Ladies from journals of fashion, shamans of lost tribes,
Or, with a secret smile, a grave *sestritsa*,
Appear among white clouds, assist.

[2]*In the 1920 war between Poland and the Soviet Union it was not uncommon for women to serve in the cavalry.*

PHILOLOGY

To the memory of Kostanty Szyrwid, S.J.,
professor of the Jesuit academy in Wilno and a
Lithuanian preacher who published in 1612 the first
Lithuanian-Latin-Polish dictionary.

He is running, lifting a little the skirt of his winter cloak.
His stockinged ankles, snow and crows.
He caught it and has it, keeps it in his mouth: a word
He has heard as a child by his native river
Near dug-outs in rushes, foot bridges, hazel bushes,
And the pointed roofs of wooden huts.
Along the arcades of the seminary to his cell,
He is running to write it down with a goose pen
Next to the register of Latin words. He coughs; logs in the fireplace,
Smoke. And the Academy Societatis Jesu
Soars above the streets and the angels
Take flesh in stone and gypsum in the mode Barocco.
With stains of sweat under armpits, how many shirts,
How many skirts covering swarthy, shadowy bellies—
And pants, generations of pants, of jerkins,
Of breeches, of cloaks and burlaps on naked skin!
Bagpipes and violins, they danced on the green,
Love meetings, touchings, teasing games.
And all of them knew the same words
Which exist, endure, though they died long ago;
As if not from the earth, from the night, from the flesh
Words arrive, but from lofty ethereal domains,
Visiting him, her, an old man, a child,
Submitted to their own law, of genitive, dative,
Obedient for centuries to a preposition.
I open a dictionary as if I summoned the souls
He enchanted into mute signs on a page,
And I try to visualize him, a lover,
To have some comfort in my mortality.

AND YET

And yet we were so like one another
With all our misery of penises and vaginas,
With the heart beating quickly in fear and ecstasy,
And a hope, a hope, a hope.

And yet we were so like one another
That lazy dragons stretching themselves in the air
Must have considered us brothers and sisters
Playing together in a sunny garden,
Only we did not know that,
Enclosed in our skins, each separately,
Not in a garden, on the bitter earth.

And yet we were so like one another
Even though every leaf of grass had its fate
Just as a sparrow on the roof, a field mouse,
And an infant that would be named John or Teresa
Was born for long happiness or shame and suffering
Once only, till the end of the world.

AT YALE

We were drinking vodka together, Brodsky, Venclova
With his beautiful Swedish girl, myself, Richard,
Near the Art Gallery, at the end of the century
Which woke up as if from a heavy slumber
And asked, in stupefaction: "What was that?
How could we? A conjunction of planets?
Or spots on the sun?"

          —For history
Is no more comprehensible. Our species
Is not ruled by any reasonable law.
The boundaries of its nature are unknown.
It is not the same as I, you, a single human.

—Thus mankind returns to its beloved pastimes
During the break. Taste and touch
Are dear to it. Cookbooks,
Recipes for perfect sex, rules
Lowering cholesterol, methods
Of quickly losing weight—that's what it needs.
It is one (from colorful magazines) body
That every morning runs along park lanes,
Touches itself in a mirror, checks its weight.
Et ça bande et ça mouille—to put it briefly.
Are we that? Does it apply to us? Yes and no.

—For, visited by dictators' dreams,
Don't we soar above them who are light-headed

And unwilling to think of the punishment that awaits
All those who are too much in love with life?

—Not so light-headed after all, they worship
In their new temples, and mortality,
Having been overcome by the craft of artists,
Comforts them in the halls of museums.

—So the time came again for adoring art.
The names of gods are forgotten, instead, the masters
Soar in the clouds, Saint Van Gogh, Matisse,
Goya, Cézanne, Hieronymus Bosch,
Together with a cluster of the smaller ones, the acolytes.
And what would they say had they stepped down on earth,
Invoked in photographs, newspapers, TV?
Where are those nights growing dense in the loneliness of a
    workshop,
Which protected, transformed the refugees from the world?

—All form—says Baudelaire—
Even the one created by man,
Is immortal. There was once an artist
Faithful and hard working. His workshop
Together with all he had painted, burned down,
He himself was executed. Nobody has heard of him.
Yet his paintings remain. On the other side of fire.

—Whenever we think of what fulfills itself
By making use of us, we are somewhat uneasy.
A form is accomplished, exists, though before it was not,
And we have nothing more to do with it. Others, generations,
Will chose what they want, accepting or destroying it.
And instead of us, real, they will need just names.

—But suppose all our internal dirt
And nuttiness and shame, a lot of shame,

Were not forgotten—would we prefer that?
They want to find in us their improved selves:
Instead of comic flaws, flaws monumentalized,
And secrets revealed, provided they are not too depressing.

"I have heard that Balzac (and who would not listen with respect to every anecdote, even the most insignificant, having to do with that genius?) one day found himself before a fine painting representing winter, a quite melancholy landscape, heavy with hoarfrost, with huts here and there, and sickly peasants. After having contemplated a small house out of which meager smoke ascended, he exclaimed: 'How beautiful it is! But what do they do in that hut? What do they think about, what are their worries? Did they have a good harvest? Certainly they have payments coming due?'

"Let people laugh at M. de Balzac. I do not know who the painter was who had the honor of making vibrate, speculate, and worry the soul of the great novelist, but it seems to me that he gave us, with his adorable naïvete, an excellent lesson in criticism. I often will appraise a painting uniquely by the sum of ideas or reveries which it brings to my mind."

—BAUDELAIRE

III

Yale Center for British Art—J.M.W. Turner (1775–1851):
"Chateaux de St. Michel, Bonneville, Savoy, 1803."

White clouds pass each other above the mountains.
And here a road in the sun, long shadows,
Low embankments, sort of a little bridge,
In a warm-brown color, the same as the tower
Of a *chateau,* which shoots up
On the dark right side, from behind the trees.
A second *chateau* far away, on the upland,
In a white blur, over a wooded slope
That descends towards the road and the hamlet in the valley
With its flock of sheep, poplars, the third
Chateau, or perhaps a romanesque church tower.
And most important: a peasant woman in a red
Skirt, a black bodice, a white
Blouse, carrying something (laundry to the stream?),
Hard to see her face—it is no more than a dot.
Yet she walked there, seen by the painter
And remained forever, only to make possible
The fulfillment of his own, revealed just to him,
Harmony in yellow, blue, and russet.

I V

To tell the truth, a rather miserable stream,
A little more abundant at the dam by the mill,
Enough to lure boys. Their angling tackle
Is quite sloppy. A branch, not a fishing rod
In the hand of the one who stands. Others slouch
Staring at their floats. Over there, in a boat
The younger ones are playing. If only blue
Were that water, but the clouds of England,
As always ragged, announce rain
And this brief clearing is the color of lead.
This is supposed to be romantic, i.e., picturesque.
Yet not for them. We are free to guess
Their patched trousers, patched shirts
As well as their dream of escaping from the village.
But let it be, after all. We recognize the right
To change everything that is sadly real
Into a composition on canvas, which has for its subject
Air. Its changeability, sudden leaps,
Cloudy turmoils, a wandering ray.
No slightest promise of Eden. Who would like to live here?
Let us pay tribute to the painter, so faithful
To bad weather, who chose it, and remains with it.

V

His name is luminosity. Whatever he saw
Would bring to him, would humbly offer
Its interior without waves, its silence, its calm,
Like a river in the haze of an early morning,
Like a mother of pearl in a black shell.
So, too, this port, in an afternoon hour
With its slumbering sails, its heat,
Where we wandered perhaps, heavy with wine,
Unbuttoning our waistcoats, for him was airy.
It revealed radiance in the disguise of a moment.
These small figures are real till today:
Here are three women, another is riding
A donkey, a man is rolling a barrel,
Horses in their collars, patient. He, holding his palette,
Called out to them, summoned them, led them away
From the poor earth of toil and bitterness
Into this velvety province of goodness.

He had his home, posthumous, in the town of New Haven,
In a white building, behind walls
Of translucent marble like turtle shell,
Which seep yellowish light on ranges of books,
Portraits and busts in bronze. There precisely
He decided to dwell when nothing any more
Would be revealed by his ashes. Though there, too,
Had he been able to touch his manuscripts
He would have been surprised by the destiny
Of such a complete change into letters, that no one
Could guess who he really was. He rebelled, screamed
And faithfully fulfilled what had been preordained,
Discovering empirically that his biography
Had been carefully arranged against his will
By powers with whom it's hard to conclude an alliance.
Has he done more evil or more good? This only
Must be important. The rest, artistry,
Does not count anyway, as they, our posterity, know
Any time the pulse is normal, breathing easy,
The day sunny, and a rosy tongue
Checks in a little mirror the dense carmine of the lip.

THE THISTLE, THE NETTLE

Let the sad terrestrials remember me,
recognize me and salute: the thistle and the tall nettle,
and the childhood enemy, belladonna.
O. V. DE L. MILOSZ
"Les Terrains Vagues"

The thistle, the nettle, the burdock, and belladonna
Have a future. Theirs are wastelands
And rusty railroad tracks, the sky, silence.

Who shall I be for men many generations later?
When, after the clamor of tongues, the award goes to silence?

I was to be redeemed by the gift of arranging words
But must be prepared for an earth without grammar,

For the thistle, the nettle, the burdock, the belladonna,
And a small wind above them, a sleepy cloud, silence.

RECONCILIATION

Late, the time of humbling reconciliation
With himself, arrived for him.
"Yes"—he said—"I was created
To be a poet and nothing more.
I did not know anything else to do,
Greatly ashamed but unable to change my fate."

The poet: one who constantly thinks of something else.
His absentmindedness drives his people to despair.
Maybe he does not even have any human feelings.

But, after all, why should it not be so?
In human diversity a mutation, variation
Is also needed. Let us visit the poet
In his little house in a somewhat faded suburb
Where he raises rabbits, prepares vodka with herbs,
And records on tape his hermetic verses.

ABODE

The grass between the tombs is intensely green.
From steep slopes a view onto the bay,
Onto islands and cities below. The sunset
Grows garish, slowly fades. At dusk
Light prancing creatures. A doe and a fawn
Are here, as every evening, to eat flowers
Which people brought for their beloved dead.

A NEW PROVINCE

You would like to hear how it is in old age?
Certainly, not much is known about that country
Till we land there ourselves, with no right to return.

1. I looked around. That it befell others,
This I can understand, but why me?
What do we have in common? Wrinkled, grayhaired,
With their canes they shuffle along, no one is expecting them.
Perhaps a young girl sees me the same way,
Though I see myself differently in the mirror.

2. Don't talk of peace. Dragged against my will,
Afraid of being abandoned any moment
By him who every day adorned the world with colors,
Put oil on my muscles, and dictated words:
Eros has never before seemed to me so mighty
And the earth of new generations so eternal.

3. How to have peace? So many faces,
They lived and vanished. "Where are you?"
I ask and try to remember
The shape of lips, of eyelids, a warm touch.
But with every new day memory is less and less eager.
So, man, I say to myself, you want to be free of dreams?

4. The course of my dying seems to me amusing.
Weakness of legs, the heart pounding, hard to go uphill.
Myself beside my refractory body.

In the clarity of my mind, as in a mountain nest.
And yet humiliated by difficulty in breathing,
Vanquished by the loss of my hair and teeth.

5. I acquired wisdom, I drink a late wine,
Truth about others and truth about myself.
Often in despair, and I ask now why.
So what if I was lame and uncertain?
Life got fulfilled, in a better or worse manner,
And a garden of forgiveness gathered all of us.

6. I would not like to be young, though I'm envious.
They do not ever know how happy they are.
They should greet a sunrise with hymns,
Compose every day a song of songs.
Yet I could not be free from myself,
Again I would get entangled in my fate and genes.
It's better that such misery is given only once.

7. I visit regions unknown until now,
Of which there is no word in learned books.
A thousand-year-old tree lasts only one day,
A butterfly is stopped in the air for ever,
A little Roman girl in an atrium flashes and disappears
At a dark turn of time without dates.
How oddly they are divided, those two tribes:
Women learning about the comic shames of men,
Men learning about the comic shames of women.
Under the feet of passersby, kings: dried-up insects,
Rue de la Vrillère, real, as long as Kot Jelenski was alive.
Once he said: "I will take you to the tomb of Cleopatra,"
And pointed it out, "Here you are," as we stood in the Passage
   Vivienne.

*(According to a persistent Parisian legend, Napoleon brought from Egypt
the mummy of Cleopatra and, not knowing what to do with it, officials buried
it in the present Passage Vivienne).*

8. *Mavet, mors, mirtis, thanatos, smrt.*
And thus it ends, the state of affairs,
All I used to list as my own.
And thus it ends, the state of mind.
Absolute cold. How will I pass through that door?
I search for what is most strongly opposed to *smrt.*
I think it is music. Of the Baroque.

9.—Oh, if only what I beg for would come true!
I would give for it half of my life!
And later it comes true. Followed by bitterness and pity.
So don't beg, mortals! You will be heard.

10. Poetry will remain after you. You were a great poet.
—But in fact, I have known only a chase.
As then, when I was awakened by quacking, gaggling in a
    farm yard
And the garish sun called me to run
Barefoot, on a still wet blackness of paths.
Was it not like that many years later, when I would start up
Every morning, knowing that so much was to be discovered
In a wilderness engraved by my pen?
I had to find a core that makes all things real,
Always hoping to reach it the next day.

11. Poetry will remain after you. A few verses, durable.
—Possibly, but that's not a strong consolation.
Who would ever have believed that the only remedy for sorrow
Would prove to be both acrid and not too effective.

12. "I walk in the disguise of an old, fat woman,"
Wrote Anna Kamienska shortly before her death.
Yes, I know. We are a lofty flame
Not identical with a clay jar. So let us write with her hand:
"Slowly I am withdrawing from my body."

(Two poets appear, girls seventeen years old.
One of them is she. They are still in high school.
They came from Lublin to a master. That is, me.

We sit in a Warsaw apartment with a view onto fields.
Janka serves tea. Politely, we crunch cookies.
I don't talk about the graves in an empty lot close by.)

13. I would prefer to be able to say: "I am satiated,
What is given to taste in this life, I have tasted."
But I am like someone in a window who draws aside a curtain
To look at a feast he does not comprehend.

READING THE NOTEBOOK OF
ANNA KAMIENSKA

Reading her, I realized how rich she was and myself, how poor.
Rich in love and suffering, in crying and dreams and prayer.
She lived among her own people who were not very happy but
    supported each other,
And were bound by a pact between the dead and the living
    renewed at the graves.
She was gladdened by herbs, wild roses, pines, potato fields
And the scents of the soil, familiar since childhood.
She was not an eminent poet. But that was just:
A good person will not learn the wiles of art.

YOUTH

Your unhappy and silly youth.
Your arrival from the provinces to the city.
Misted-over windowpanes of streetcars,
Restless misery of the crowd.
Your dread when you entered a place too expensive.
But everything was too expensive. Too high.
Those people must have noticed your crude manners,
Your outmoded clothes, and your awkwardness.

There were none who would stand by you and say,

You are a handsome boy,
You are strong and healthy,
Your misfortunes are imaginary.

You would not have envied a tenor in an overcoat of camel
    hair
Had you guessed his fear and known how he would die.

She, the red-haired, because of whom you suffered tortures,
So beautiful she seemed to you, is a doll in fire,
You don't understand what she screams with her lips of a
    clown.

The shapes of hats, the cut of robes, faces in the mirrors,
You will remember unclearly like something from
    long ago
Or like what remains from a dream.

The house you approached trembling,
The apartment that dazzled you—
Look, on this spot the cranes clear the rubble.

In your turn you will have, possess, secure,
Able to be proud at last, when there is no reason.

Your wishes will be fulfilled, you will gape then
At the essence of time, woven of smoke and mist,

An iridescent fabric of lives that last one day,
Which rises and falls like an unchanging sea.

Books you have read will be of use no more.
You searched for an answer but lived without answer.

You will walk in the streets of southern cities,
Restored to your beginnings, seeing again in rapture
The whiteness of a garden after the first night of snow.

IN COMMON

What is good? Garlic. A leg of lamb on a spit.
Wine with a view of boats rocking in a cove.
A starry sky in August. A rest on a mountain peak.

What is good? After a long drive water in a pool and a sauna.
Lovemaking and falling asleep, embraced, your legs touching hers.
Mist in the morning, translucent, announcing a sunny day.

I am submerged in everything that is common to us, the living.
Experiencing this earth for them, in my flesh.
Walking past the vague outline of skyscrapers? anti-temples?
In valleys of beautiful, though poisoned, rivers.

A PHOTOGRAPH

Few tasks more difficult
Than to write a treatise
On a man who looks
At an old photograph.

Why he does it
Is incomprehensible
And his feelings
Cannot be explained.

Seemingly it's simple:
She was his love.
But here precisely
Questions begin.

If she is tangible
So strongly present
In her skin and her dress,
Her nails and hair,

Was she then a cloud
Or a river wave,
And did she return
To nonexistence?

Or, on the contrary
Is she still a substance,
A thing with duration
Separate and eternal?

We are taught in schools
About the unity of life—
Of plants and protozoa,
Of insects and humans—

Which incessantly
Renews itself and falls
Into our common
Fatherland—abyss.

Thence comes compassion
For every living thing—
Without distinction
Between human and nonhuman.

But how, then, to preserve
That golden privilege
Of an immortality
Given to us only?

Already we hear
Theologians say:
"Being disintegrates,
Substance escapes us."

Meditating over
Her photograph
He repeats to himself
Words of a Zen poet:

"What is our I?
A short-lived ball
Of earth and water,
Of fire and wind."

And, inconceivable,
He addresses her,

Perfectly certain
That she hears him:

"O maiden of the Lord,
Promised to me,
With whom I was to have
At least twelve children,

"Obtain for me the grace
Of your strong faith.
We living are too weak
Without your assistance.

You are for me now
The mystery of time
i.e., of a person
Changing and the same,

Who runs in the garden
Fragrant after the rain
With a ribbon in your hair
And lives in the beyond.

You see how I try
To reach with words
What matters most
And how I fail.

Though perhaps this moment
When you are so close
Is precisely your help
And an act of forgiveness."

LASTINGNESS

That was in a big city, no matter what country, what language,
A long time ago (blessed be the gift
Of spinning a tale out of a trifle,
In the street, in a car—I write it down not to lose it).
Perhaps not a trifle, a crowded night café
Where every evening a famous chanteuse used to sing.
I was sitting with others in smoke, a clatter of beer glasses.
Ties, officers' uniforms, deep décolletés of women,
Wild music of their folklore, probably from the mountains.
And that singer, her throat, a pulsating stem,
Her dancing movement, the black of her hair, white of her
    skin,
The imagined scent of her perfumes.
What have I learned since, what have I discovered?
States, customs, lives, gone.
No trace of her or of that café.
And only her shade with me, her frailty, beauty, always.

EITHER-OR

If God incarnated himself in man, died and rose from the dead,
All human endeavors deserve attention
Only to the degree that they depend on this,
I.e., acquire meaning thanks to this event.
We should think of this by day and by night.
Every day, for years, ever stronger and deeper.
And most of all about how human history is holy
And how every deed of ours becomes a part of it,
Is written down for ever, and nothing is ever lost.
Because our kind was so much elevated
Priesthood should be our calling
Even if we do not wear liturgical garments.
We should publicly testify to the divine glory
With words, music, dance, and every sign.

If what is proclaimed by Christianity is a fiction
And what we are taught in schools,
In newspapers and TV is true:
That the evolution of life is an accident,
As is an accident the existence of man,
And that his history goes from nowhere to nowhere,
Our duty is to draw conclusions
From our thinking about the innumerable generations
Who lived and died deluding themselves,
Ready to renounce their natural needs for no reason,
To wait for a posthumous verdict, every day afraid
That for licking clean a pot of jam they go to eternal torment.

If a poor degenerate animal
Could have reached so far in his fantasies
And peopled the air with radiant beings,
Rocky chasms with crowds of devils,
The consequences of it must be, indeed, serious.
We should go and proclaim without cease
And remind people at every step of what we are:
That our capacity for self-delusion has no limits
And that anybody who believes anything is mistaken.
The only gesture worthy of respect is to complain of our
    transience,
Of the one end for all our attachments and hopes,
As if by threatening indifferent Heaven,
We fulfilled that which distinguishes our species.

Not at all! Why either-or?
For centuries men and gods have lived together,
Supplications have been made for health or a successful journey.
Not that one should constantly meditate on who Jesus was.
What can we, ordinary people, know of the Mystery?
Not worse than our neighbors and kin,
We pay homage to it every Sunday.
It is better that not everyone is called to priesthood.
Some are for prayers, others for their sins.
It's a pity that their sermons are always so boring
As if they themselves no more understood.
Let scientists describe the origin of life.
Perhaps it's true, but is all that for human beings?

Day follows night, trees bloom in the spring—
Such discoveries are certainly less harmful.
May we not care about what awaits us after death
But here on earth look for salvation,
Trying to do good within our limits,
Forgiving the mortals their imperfection. Amen.

TWO POEMS

The two poems placed here together contradict each other. The first renounces any dealing with problems which for centuries have been tormenting the minds of theologians and philosophers; it chooses a moment and the beauty of the earth as observed on one of the Caribbean islands. The second, just the opposite, voices anger because people do not want to remember, and live as if nothing happened, as if horror were not hiding just beneath the surface of their social arrangements.

I alone know that the assent to the world in the first poem masks much bitterness and that its serenity is perhaps more ironic than it seems. And the disagreement with the world in the second results from anger which is a stronger stimulus than an invitation to a philosophical dispute. But let it be, the two poems taken together testify to my contradictions, since the opinions voiced in one and the other are equally mine.

Conversation with Jeanne

Let us not talk philosophy, drop it, Jeanne.
So many words, so much paper, who can stand it.
I told you the truth about my distancing myself.
I've stopped worrying about my misshapen life.
It was no better and no worse than the usual human tragedies.

For over thirty years we have been waging our dispute
As we do now, on the island under the skies of the tropics.
We flee a downpour, in an instant the bright sun again,
And I grow dumb, dazzled by the emerald essence of the leaves.

We submerge in foam at the line of the surf,
We swim far, to where the horizon is a tangle of banana bush,
With little windmills of palms.
And I am under accusation: That I am not up to my oeuvre,
That I do not demand enough from myself,
As I could have learned from Karl Jaspers,
That my scorn for the opinions of this age grows slack.

I roll on a wave and look at white clouds.

You are right, Jeanne, I don't know how to care about the
    salvation of my soul.
Some are called, others manage as well as they can.
I accept it, what has befallen me is just.
I don't pretend to the dignity of a wise old age.
Untranslatable into words, I chose my home in what is now,
In things of this world, which exist and, for that reason, delight us:
Nakedness of women on the beach, coppery cones of their breasts,

Hibiscus, alamanda, a red lily, devouring
With my eyes, lips, tongue, the guava juice, the juice of *la prune*
   de Cythère,
Rum with ice and syrup, lianas-orchids
In a rain forest, where trees stand on the stilts of their roots.

Death, you say, mine and yours, closer and closer,
We suffered and this poor earth was not enough.
The purple-black earth of vegetable gardens
Will be here, either looked at or not.
The sea, as today, will breathe from its depths.
Growing small, I disappear in the immense, more and more free.

Guadeloupe

A Poem for the End of the Century

When everything was fine
And the notion of sin had vanished
And the earth was ready
In universal peace
To consume and rejoice
Without creeds and utopias,

I, for unknown reasons,
Surrounded by the books
Of prophets and theologians,
Of philosophers, poets,
Searched for an answer,
Scowling, grimacing,
Waking up at night, muttering at dawn.

What oppressed me so much
Was a bit shameful.
Talking of it aloud
Would show neither tact nor prudence.
It might even seem an outrage
Against the health of mankind.

Alas, my memory
Does not want to leave me
And in it, live beings
Each with its own pain,
Each with its own dying,
Its own trepidation.

Why then innocence
On paradisal beaches,
An impeccable sky
Over the church of hygiene?
Is it because *that*
Was long ago?

To a saintly man
—So goes an Arab tale—
God said somewhat maliciously:
"Had I revealed to people
How great a sinner you are,
They could not praise you."

"And I," answered the pious one,
"Had I unveiled to them
How merciful you are,
They would not care for you."

To whom should I turn
With that affair so dark
Of pain and also guilt
In the structure of the world,
If either here below
Or over there on high
No power can abolish
The cause and the effect?

Don't think, don't remember
The death on the cross,
Though everyday He dies,
The only one, all-loving,
Who without any need
Consented and allowed
To exist all that is,
Including nails of torture.

Totally enigmatic.
Impossibly intricate.
Better to stop speech here.
This language is not for people.
Blessed be jubilation.
Vintages and harvests.
Even if not everyone
Is granted serenity.

Berkeley

SPIDER

The thread with which he landed stuck to the bottom of the
  bathtub
And he desperately tries to walk on the glossy white
But not one of his thrashing legs gets a hold
On that surface so unlike anything in Nature.
I do not like spiders. Between me and them there is enmity.
I have read a lot about their habits
Which are loathsome to me. In a web
I have seen the quick run, a lethal stabbing
With poison that, in some species,
Is dangerous also for us. Now I take a look
And leave him there. Instead of running water
To end this unpleasantness. For, after all, what can we,
People, do except not to harm?
Not to pour toxic powder on the road of marching ants,
Save stupid moths rushing to the light
By putting a windowpane between them and the kerosene lamp
By which I used to write. Name this at last,
I tell myself: Reluctance to think to the end
Is lifesaving for the living. Could lucid consciousness
Bear everything that in every minute,
Simultaneously, occurs on the earth?
Not to harm. Stop eating fish and meat.
Let oneself be castrated, like Tiny, a cat innocent
Of the drownings of kittens every day in our city.

The Cathari were right: Avoid the sin of conception
(For either you kill your seed and will be tormented by conscience
Or you will be responsible for a life of pain).

45

My house has two bathrooms. I leave the spider
In an unused tub and go back to my work
Which consists in building diminutive boats
More wieldy and speedy than those in our childhood,
Good for sailing beyond the borderline of time.

Next day I see my spider:
Dead, rolled into a black dot on the glittering white.

I think with envy of the dignity that befell Adam
Before whom creatures of field and forest paraded
To receive names from him. How much he was elevated
Above everything that runs and flies and crawls.

FAR AWAY

Great love makes a great grief.
SKARGA

I

The chronicler is breathing, his heart is beating.
This is rare among chroniclers, for they are usually dead.
He tries to describe the earth as he remembers it
I.e., to describe on that earth his first love,
A girl bearing some ordinary name
From whom he will never again receive a letter
And who astonishes him by her strong existence
So that she seems to dictate what he writes.

It happened a long, long time ago.
In a city which was like an oratorio
Shooting with its ornate towers up to the sky
Into the white clouds, from among green hills.
We were growing there next to each other, unaware of it,
In the same legend: about a subterranean river
Nobody has ever seen, about a basilisk
Under a medieval tower, about a secret passage
Which led from the city to a remote island
With the ruins of a castle in the middle of the lake.
Every spring we took the same delight in the river:
Ice is breaking, it flows, and look, ferry boats
Painted in blue and green stripes,
And majestic raft trains drift to the sawmills.

In the sun of April we were walking in the crowd.
Expectation was timid, nameless.
And only now, when every "he loves me, loves me not"
Is fulfilled, when ridicule and grief
Are alike and I am at one

47

With those girls and boys, saying farewell,
I realize how strong their love was for their city.
Though they were unaware, it was to last them a lifetime.
They were destined to live through the loss of their country,
To search for a souvenir, a sign, something that does not perish.
And had I to offer a gift to her, I would choose this:
I would place her among the dreams of architecture,
There, where St. Ann and the Bernardins,
St. John and the Missionaries meet the sky.

2

In the scent of savory, there where the path
Winds down towards the alders and the rushes
Of a small lake, in the sun, beehives.
The unchanging bees of our forest country
Work, as always, on tne day we perish.

She was quick. She shouted: "Now!
No time to lose!"—and they grabbed the children,
They ran that path, from the house, by the alders, into the
    swamp.
The soldiers came out of the birch grove, were surrounding
    the house,
They had left their truck in the woods, so as not to scare
    people away.
"They did not think to let the dog loose,
It would have certainly led them to us."
Thus our country was ending, still generously
Protective with its osiers, mosses, wild rosemaries.
Long trains were moving eastward, towards Asia,
With the laments of those who knew they would not return.

Bees fly, heavy, to their mead breweries,
White clouds drift slowly, reflected in the lake.
Our heritage will be handed to unknown people.
Will they respect the hives, nasturtiums by the porch,
Carefully weeded patches, the slanting apple trees?

3

But yes, the restaurant's name was "A Cozy Nook."
How could I have forgotten! Does it mean
I did not want to remember? And the city was falling
Into its sleepy moulting, into a long season
Of people I could not imagine. It hardly, hardly
Returns. Why in my poems is there so little
Autobiography? Where did it come from, the idea
To hide what is my own as if it were sick?
Then, in the "Cozy Nook" I was still one
Of the gentlemen, students, and officers, before whom
Little Matthew's waiters would put a carafe
Of vodka straight from the ice, misty with dew,
And to be adult made you proud,
Just as you felt proud coming of good stock.
This took place in a Europe of swamps and pine forests,
Of horse carts creaking on sandy highways.
Little Matthew, obliging, circulated among the tables.
Was he to become an informer? Or has he gone
To a gulag on one of the Siberian rivers?

4

How stupid is the business of the State.
I should not write about it and yet I do.
For, after all, one pities people.

Here where I live they buy and sell
Every hour of the day and night.
In halls sprinkled with bluish light they heap
Fruits brought from five continents,
Fish and meats from the East and West,
Snails and oysters summoned against the clock,
Liquors fermented in sultry valleys.
I have nothing against the Polynesias in shop windows,
Against a virgin nature at a modest price.
And if I object, I keep it to myself, it's simpler.

I am not from here. From a remote province,
From a remote continent
Where I had learned the nature of the State.

By a river in the evening, our choral singing.
We were living beyond marshes, beyond woods,
Thirty kilometers from the nearest railway station,
In manors, yeomen's lodges, farmhouses, hamlets.
Our singing was about division: this here
Is ours, that over there is alien, here poverty, there wealth,
Here ploughing, there trading, here virtue, there sin,
Here faithfulness to the ancestors, there treason,
And the worst of all, if one should sell his forest.
The oaks stood there for ages, now they were falling

With thunderous echoes, so that the earth trembled.
And then the road to our parish church
Led no more through shade with songs of birds
But through empty and silent clearings,
And that was like a presage of every kind of loss.
We implored the protection of the Miraculous Virgin,
We accompanied organ music with Latin chants.
Generation after generation we lived against the State
Which would not overcome us either with threat or punishment.
Till a perfect State appeared on the earth.

The state is perfect if it takes away
From every man his name, sex, dress, and manner,
And carries them at dawn, insane with fear,
Where, no one knows, to steppes, deserts,
So that its power is revealed
And, wallowing in their filth,
Hungry, humiliated, men renounce their right.
What did we know of this? Nothing at all.
And later on there were none among us
Who would be able to tell the world about this new knowledge.
The age passes, memory passes. Nobody will find
Letters begging for help, graves without crosses.

INHERITOR

Listen, perhaps you will hear me, young man.
Noon. Crickets sing as they did for us
A hundred years ago. A white cloud passes,
Its shadow runs beneath it, the river glitters.
Your nakedness. The echo
Of a tongue unknown to you, here, in the air,
Our words addressed to you, gentle and guitless
Son of invaders. You do not know
What happened here. You do not seek
Faith and hope as they were practiced here,
You walk by smashed stones with the fragments of a name.
Yet this water in the sun, the scent of calamus,
The same ecstasy of discovering things
Unite us. You will find again
The sacredness they tried to expel forever.
Something returns, invisible, frail and shy,
Adoring, without name, and yet fearless.
After our despair, your hottest blood,
Your young and avid eyes succeed us.
Our heir. Now we are allowed to go.
Again, listen. Echo. Faint. Fainter.

GATHERING APRICOTS

In the sun, while there, below, over the bay
Only clouds of white mist wander, fleeting,
And the range of hills is grayish on the blue,
Apricots, the whole tree full of them, in the dark leaves,
Glimmer, yellow and red, bringing to mind
The garden of Hesperides and apples of Paradise.
I reach for a fruit and suddenly feel the presence
And put aside the basket and say: "It's a pity
That you died and cannot see these apricots,
While I celebrate this undeserved life."

COMMENTARY

Alas, I did not say what I should have.
I submitted fog and chaos to a distillation.
That other kingdom of being or non-being
Is always with me and makes itself heard
With thousands of calls, screams, complaints,
And she, the one to whom I turned,
Is perhaps but a leader of a chorus.
What happened only once does not stay in words.
Countries disappeared and towns and circumstances.
Nobody will be able to see her face.
And form itself as always is a betrayal.

MEDITATION

With an ancient love worn down by pity, anger, and solitude.
O. V. DE L. MILOSZ

Lord, it is quite possible that people, while praising you, were
    mistaken.
You were not a ruler on a throne to whom from here below
    prayers and the smoke of incense ascend.
The throne they imagined was empty and you smiled bitterly
Seeing that they turn to you with the hope
That you will protect their crops from hail and their bodies
    from illness,
That you save them from pestilence, hunger, fire and war.
A wanderer, camping by invisible waters, you would keep a
    little flame hardly visible in darkness.
And sitting by it, pensive, you would shake your head.
So much you wanted to help them, glad any time you succeeded,
You felt compassion for them, forgiving them their mistake,
Their falsity, of which they were aware, pretending they did not
    know it,
And even their ugliness, as they gathered in their churches.
Lord, my heart is full of admiration and I want to talk with you,
For I am sure you understand me, in spite of my contradictions.
It seems to me that now I learned at last what it means to love people
And why love is worn down by loneliness, pity, and anger.
It is enough to reflect strongly and persistently on one life,
On a certain woman, for instance, as I am doing now
To perceive the greatness of those—weak—creatures
Who are able to be honest, brave in misfortune, and patient till
    the end.
What can I do more, Lord, than to meditate on all that
And stand before you in the attitude of an implorer
For the sake of their heroism asking: Admit us to your glory.

ON A BEACH

The sea breaks on the sands, I listen to its *szum* and *szum* and close my eyes,

Here on this European shore, in the fullness of summer, after the big wars of the century.

The brows of new generations are innocent, yet marked.

Often in a crowd a face resembling—he could be one of the destroyers

If he were born a little earlier but he doesn't know it.

Chosen, as his father was, though not called.

Under my eyelids I keep their eternally young cities.

The shouts of their music, the rock pulsating, I am searching for the core of my thought.

Is it only this, inexpressible, and what's left is to mumble every day "ah"—:

The irretrievable, indifferent, eternal passing away?

Is it pity and anger because after the ecstasy and despair and hope beings similar to gods are swallowed by oblivion?

Because in the sea's szums and silences one hears nothing about a division into the just and the wicked?

Or was I pursued by images of those who were alive for a day, an hour, a moment, under the skies?

So much, and now the peace of defeat, for my verse preserved so little?

Or perhaps I have only heard myself whispering: "Epilogue, epilogue"?

Prophecies of my youth fulfilled but not in the way one expected.

The morning is back, and flowers are gathered in the cool of the garden by a loving hand.

A flock of pigeons soars above the valley. They turn and change color flying along the mountains.

Same glory of ordinary days and milk in a jug and crisp cherries.

And yet down below, in the very brushwood of existence, it lurks and crawls,

Recognizable by the fluttering dread of small creatures, it, implacable, steel-gray nothingness.

.   .   .

I open my eyes, a red sail leans on a wave which is blue in the gaudy sun.

Just before me a boy tests the water with his foot, and suddenly I notice he is not like others.

Not crippled, yet he has the movements of a cripple and the head of a retarded child.

His father looks after him, that handsome man sitting there on a boulder.

A sensation of my neighbor's misfortune pierces me and I begin to comprehend

In this dark age the bond of our common fate and a compassion more real than I was inclined to confess.

RETURN

In my old age I decided to visit places where I wandered long ago
in my early youth.

I recognized smells, the outline of postglacial hills and oval-shaped
lakes.

I forced my way through a thicket where a park was once, but
I did not find the traces of the lanes.

Standing on the shore while the wave shimmered lightly as it
did then, I was incomprehensibly the same, incomprehensibly
different.

And yet I will not repudiate you, unlucky youngster,
nor dismiss the reasons for your sufferings as foolish.

He to whom the pitiless truth of existence is suddenly unveiled,
cannot but ask: How can it be?

How can it be, such an order of the world—unless it was created
by a cruel demiurge?

There is nothing to esteem in the fattened wisdom of adults, and
acquiescence trained in slyness is disgraceful.

Let us honor a protest against the immutable law and honor
revolvers in the hands of adolescents when they refuse to
participate for ever.

And then—was it not like this?—a woman's hand covers our eyes and a gift is offered: brown shields of her breasts, the ebony tuft of her belly.

How the heart beats! Only for me such happiness? Nobody knows, nobody guesses the golden marvel of her body.

Only for you? I nod and look at the lake—only for you, and thus since the millennia, so that the beauty of the earth be exalted.

And now, after a long life, grown slyly just and made wise by mere searching, I ask whether all that was worthwhile.

When doing good we also do evil, the balances evening out, that's all, and a blindly accomplished destiny.

Nobody here, I did not feel troubled spirits flying by, only the wind was bending the bullrushes, so I could not say to her:
You see.

Somehow I waded through; I am grateful that I was not submitted to tests beyond my strength, and yet I still think that the human soul belongs to the anti-world.

Which is real as this one is real and horrible and comic and senseless.

I toiled and kept choosing the opposite: a perfect Nature lifted above chaos and transience, a changeless garden on the other side of time.

*   *   *

Large finger-like leaves of an Hawaiian fern
Seen against the sun and my joy
At the thought that they will be when I am no more.
I try to grasp what that joy signifies.

GOOD NIGHT

No duties. I don't have to be profound.
I don't have to be artistically perfect.
Or sublime. Or edifying.
I just wander. I say: "You were running,
That's fine. It was the thing to do."
And now the music of the worlds transforms me.
My planet enters a different house.
Trees and lawns become more distinct.
Philosophies one after another go out.
Everything is lighter yet not less odd.
Sauces, wine vintages, dishes of meat.
We talk a little of district fairs,
Of travels in a covered wagon with a cloud of dust behind,
Of how rivers once were, what the scent of calamus is.
That's better than examining one's private dreams.
And meanwhile it has arrived. It's here, invisible.
Who can guess how it got here, everywhere.
Let others take care of it. Time for me to play hooky.
Buena notte. Ciao. Farewell.

DECEMBER I

The vineyard country, russet, reddish, carmine-brown in this season.
A blue outline of hills above a fertile valley.
It's warm as long as the sun does not set, in the shade cold returns.
A strong sauna and then swimming in a pool surrounded by trees.
Dark redwoods, transparent pale-leaved birches.
In their delicate network, a sliver of the moon.
I describe this for I have learned to doubt philosophy
And the visible world is all that remains.

DANTE

To be so poor. No heaven, no abyss,
A revolving wheel of seasons.
Humans under the stars
Walk and disintegrate
Into ash or a stellar dust.
Molecular machines work faultlessly, self-propelled.
Lilium columbianum opens its tiger-striped flowers
And in an instant they shrink into a sticky pulp.
Trees grow up, straight up in the air.

O alchemist Alighieri, how distant
From your harmony is that crazy sequence,
That cosmos at which I wonder and in which I vanish,
Not knowing anything about the immortal soul,
My eyes riveted to unpopulated screens.

Colorful slippers, ribbons, rings
Are sold as always on the bridge at Arno.
I choose a gift for Theodora,
Elvire or Julia, whatever the name
Of her with whom I sleep and play chess.
In a bathroom, sitting at the edge of a tub
I look at her, flesh-colored in greenish water.
Not at her, at nakedness, abstraction,
Which makes our bodies not our own.

Ideas, words, emotions abandon us
As if our ancestors were a different species.

It's more and more difficult to compose love songs,
Wedding canzones, a solemn music.

And only, as once for you, this remains real:
La concreata e perpetua sete,
The inborn and the perpetual desire
Del deiformo regno—for a God-like domain,
A realm or a kingdom. There is my home.
I cannot help it. I pray for light,
For the inside of the eternal pearl, *L'etterna margarita.*

MEANING

—When I die, I will see the lining of the world.
The other side, beyond bird, mountain, sunset.
The true meaning, ready to be decoded.
What never added up will add up,
What was incomprehensible will be comprehended.

—And if there is no lining to the world?
If a thrush on a branch is not a sign,
But just a thrush on the branch? If night and day
Make no sense following each other?
And on this earth there is nothing except this earth?

—Even if that is so, there will remain
A word wakened by lips that perish,
A tireless messenger who runs and runs
Through interstellar fields, through the revolving galaxies,
And calls out, protests, screams.

KAZIA

A two-horse wagon was covered with tarpaulin stretched on boughs of hazel and in that manner we had been voyaging a couple of days, while my eyes kept starting out of my head from curiosity. Especially when we left the flat region of fields and woods for a country of hills and many lakes, of which I was to learn later that it was shaped thus by a glacier. That country revealed to me something not named, what might be called today a peaceful husbandry of man on the earth: the smoke of villages, cattle coming back from pasture, mowers with their scythes cutting oats and after-grasses, here and there a rowboat near the shore, rocked gently by a wave. Undoubtedly these things existed also elsewhere, but here they were somehow condensed into one modest space of everyday rituals and labors.

We were hospitably received for the night in a manor by a lake. My memory stops at the very border of returning there but cannot cross it and the name of the place does not appear, nor the name of our hosts, nothing except the name, Kazia, of that little girl at whom I looked, about whom I thought something, though how she looked I do not know anymore, all I know is that she was wearing a sailor's collar.

And so it is, against expectation, that Kazia or another girl, a complete stranger, accompanies us for years and we constantly ask ourselves what happened to her. For, after all, we are able, by concentrating our attention, to raise her, so to say, to the square and to make her important to us disinterestedly, since nothing sentimental colors our imaginings. This is a meditation on one of our contemporaries, how she did not choose a place or time to be born into such and such family. There is no help, I entangle her in everything that has happened since that moment, thus, the history of the century, of the country, of that region. Let us assume that she married, had a child, then was deported to Asia, starving, infected with lice, tried to save herself and her child, worked hard, discovering a dimension of existence which is better left in silence, for our notions of decency and morality have nothing to do with it. Let us assume she learned about the death of her husband in a gulag, found herself in Iran, had two husbands more, lived successively in Africa, in England, in America. And the house by the lake followed her in her dreams. Of course in my fantasies I imagine a day and a place of our meeting as two adults, which has never occurred, perhaps our affair, her nakedness, her hair, dark I am pretty certain, our basic resemblance, of a couple having the same tribe, language, manners. We have been paying too much attention to what separates people; in truth we could have been, we, the two of us, married, and it would have been fine, and our biographies would have faded in human memory as they fade now, when I have no idea what she really felt and thought, and am unable to describe it.

A PHILOSOPHER'S HOME

Pondering over the testimony of his predecessors he knew that he was entering the age of the mind. When, as they say, blood circulates more slowly, when outbursts of anger and desire are rarer and rarer, while our own existence is accepted without vain regrets, the time has arrived for liberating ourselves from the rituals of our contemporaries. Their judgements amused him. They were not founded on anything, heard once and repeated because of fashion, i.e., animal warmth. The names of their great were losing their appeal. Highly regarded works could not, at a new reading, conceal their blemishes and seemed mediocre.

Deprived of many illusions, the mind abandoned itself the more eagerly to voyaging amidst the phenomena, i.e., all things that appear to us by the intermediary of the senses. The door of a car slams and a woman in a green overcoat quickly runs up a few steps; votive candles are lit on the terrace of a Shintoist temple; a barman serves a drink to a man in a crumpled hat; a scream "ouch!" at hurting herself with a needle; at a florist, the cut ends of stems while the hand of the seller composes a bouquet; lean dogs in refuse-heaped outskirts under the smoke of mills; glittering multi-colored lines of freeways in a metropolis; the feet of a homeless man sticking out in a corridor of a metro. Circumstances and coincidences, such as are or might have been, all those "because ofs," "if nots," and "if onlys." Also, an infinite number of theories, theses, beliefs, hypotheses, appeals, avowals in the sounds of speech, in the letters of a written language. The mind marvelled at that overflowing multiplicity: it sneaked into a secret session of the Venetian Council of Ten, participated in the invention of cuneiform writing, was entering a crusader's tent and

looking at the head of a sleeping woman, was flying over a clear-
ing on the plateau of an island where our brethren the cannibals
performed their dances.

Simultaneous multiplicity, in every minute and second of the
existence of the world, but also another kind, extending across
years, centuries, a thousand and a million years, and millions of
years. And everywhere the mind was allowed to travel; light and
fleshless, it was soaring over the earth before man, watching
eruptions of volcanoes and the pastures of dinosaurs.

Meditating on that privilege of the mind, he was astonished by
the lack of its resemblance to the body which soon would die, but
also by its, the mind's, greed which can never be satisfied. For the
more it wanted to embrace, the more those things which escaped
it grew in size. And that disparity between striving and achieving
was the source of the pious awe of philosophers, at least of the
school to which he himself wished to belong.

Is it possible, he asked himself, that this spectacle of the incredible
multitude of forms, each of them appearing in a definite point of
time, proper to it only, is it possible that this breath-taking spec-
tacle is played for nobody? Does not the mind, as it possesses a
never assuaged desire for detail, show by its very nature its affin-
ity to an absolute mind, a witness present in every moment of
space-time? Indeed, this theatre must have a spectator, even if the
actors are not aware of him, just as a blade of grass is not aware
of human eyes which look at it. Let us repeat then a maxim more
important now than at any other time: *esse* is *percipi*, to be is to
be perceived.

COMMENTARY

Philosophers have a measure of time that is different from that of
ordinary mortals. They converse with Plato, listen to the argu-
ments of Thomas Aquinas, visit Spinoza's study. The philosopher

who speaks in *A Philosopher's Home* has been, however, shaped in the first place by what surrounded him in the twentieth century. It is not difficult to notice that his gluttony for images has much in common with the eye of a movie camera, and he probably quite often travelled merely by sitting before a screen. The camera did not only provide him with pictures taken in various countries of the earth, for it plunged into the depths of the sea, into the interstellar spaces, and even reached other planets. Wherever he turned, he saw photographs of people upon the background of rural and urban landscapes, he caught and retained moments of their labors and leisure, of their loves and wars. Espying their denuded bodies, in health and beauty, in withering and illness, in starvation and in agony from wounds, in the triumphs of victory in sports. He must have also liked pornographic photographs and films which dissolve our individual features in a universally practiced activity of incomparable ludicrousness.

And books—for he undoubtedly glimpsed into the kind of books not accessible to any of his distinguished predecessors. They described and illustrated life in ancient China and ancient Egypt, Greece, the islands of Polynesia. He was becoming acquainted with the shapes of clay vats for wine, with various types of sails, with colors of wedding dresses, with the art of constructing siege-trains and making a silver handle for brushes to paint the eyelids. The history of our species opened to him as read anew from remnants of mosaics, from the contents of a tomb where the dead had reposed in silence and peace for three thousand years, from newly found poems whose authors will forever remain nameless. Or he wondered at the incessant changeability of the so-called live nature whose scenes from millennia before were described by zealous partisans of the theory of evolution.

From what he says we can also deduce that he had visited museums and galleries of art where the hand of an artist stops a year, a day, an instant and all he touched persists though it happened long ago. We may suspect him of having the habits of a stroller through galleries and guess in his reasoning the hidden passion of a collector, or the curator of an immense museum of things once seen.

Thus, paradoxically, the twentieth century directed the philosopher towards the idea of an Eye (we remember the eye in a triangle) which is the eye of a universal witness, even, who knows, of a super-curator of the universe or the owner of a movie camera absolutely perfect, for it is pointed towards everything. Even if philosophers of old meditated upon the omniscience of God, besides trying in vain to solve the riddle of Providence, no one of them chose for a point of departure certain traits of our mind intensified by technology. They would humanize the Highest, ascribing to Him human feelings and human will, but they never tried to endow Him with the passionate zeal of a photo-reporter.